Laura Zinszer
CPS / Douglass H.S.

Amelia
Earhart

JUNIOR ■ WORLD ■ BIOGRAPHIES

Amelia Earhart

LEIGH HOPE WOOD

CHELSEA JUNIORS
a division of CHELSEA HOUSE PUBLISHERS

English-language words that are italicized in the text can be found in the glossary at the back of the book.

Chelsea House Publishers

EDITORIAL DIRECTOR Richard Rennert
EXECUTIVE MANAGING EDITOR Karyn Gullen Browne
COPY CHIEF Robin James
PICTURE EDITOR Adrian G. Allen
CREATIVE DIRECTOR Robert Mitchell
ART DIRECTOR Joan Ferrigno
PRODUCTION MANAGER Sallye Scott

JUNIOR WORLD BIOGRAPHIES

SENIOR EDITOR Martin Schwabacher
SERIES DESIGN Marjorie Zaum

Staff for AMELIA EARHART
EDITORIAL ASSISTANT Erin McKenna
PICTURE RESEARCHER Sandy Jones
COVER ILLUSTRATION Janet Hamlin

3 5 7 9 8 6 4 2

Library of Congress Cataloging-in-Publication Data
Wood, Leigh Hope.
Amelia Earhart : daring aviator / Leigh Hope Wood.
  p. cm. — (Junior world biographies)
Includes bibliographical references and index.
Summary: Follows the life of the pilot who was the first woman to cross the Atlantic by herself in a plane.
  ISBN 0-7910-2294-3
  ISBN 0-7910-2299-4 (pbk.)
1. Earhart, Amelia, 1897-1937—Juvenile literature. 2. Air pilots—United States—Biography—Juvenile literature. [1.Earhart, Amelia, 1897-1937. 2. Air pilots. 3. Women—Biography.] I. Title. II. Series.
TL540.E3W66 1996
629.13'092—dc20
[B]

95-37891
CIP
AC

Contents

When Amelia Earhart took off for Europe on May 20, 1932, from Newfoundland, she was attempting to do what no woman—and only one man—had ever done before: fly alone across the Atlantic Ocean.

1

The Big Adventure

In Harbour Grace, Newfoundland, the day was ending, but a big adventure was just beginning. Dressed in a baggy leather flight suit, a pilot stepped into the cockpit of a red and gold single-engine plane. The pilot started the engine and nodded. Two mechanics pulled the blocks away from the plane's wheels, and the aircraft taxied down the runway. The plane got off the ground gracefully and headed east.

It was May 20, 1932. Less than three decades had passed since Orville and Wilbur

Wright's famous 12-second flight at Kitty Hawk, North Carolina. And only five years before, in 1927, Charles Lindbergh had made the first *solo* flight across the Atlantic. No one had followed him—until Amelia Earhart. If she succeeded, she would be the first woman to make the trip alone.

Earhart felt ready for this challenge. She had been flying for 12 years and had logged more than 1,000 hours in the air. In 1928, she had made a solo round-trip flight across the United States. But the 2,000-mile Atlantic crossing would be the climax of her career thus far.

It was a dangerous trip. The North Atlantic was known for its rapidly changing weather, and forecasters depended on reports from ships to make predictions. There were no satellites to tell pilots whether clear skies or clouds lay ahead.

Earhart was flying at about 12,000 feet when she glanced at the instrument panel and noticed that something was wrong. The needle on the *altimeter* was circling the dial. It was broken. Without it, she could not tell how far above the ground she was flying.

Next, the moon disappeared behind some clouds, and the plane was hit by thunderstorms. Earhart pulled the nose up and gained *altitude*. She hoped to get above the clouds, but the plane began to lose speed. As it climbed, the air was getting colder, and ice was forming on the wings.

In order to get into warmer air, Earhart put the plane into a spin and dropped several thousand feet straight down. Suddenly, she saw waves breaking right below her. She pulled the plane up in a hurry.

At about 11:30 P.M., Earhart saw flames coming through a broken weld in the engine's exhaust outlet. If that section separated, the plane would probably be torn apart. She reasoned, however, that the metal was thick and heavy enough to last. It was best to continue on: if she returned to Newfoundland and landed with all her fuel, the plane could catch fire.

At dawn, the storm lifted, and the sun almost blinded the weary pilot. Earhart dipped below the clouds. Her hands were aching, and she was exhausted.

During the last two hours of the journey, the plane began to vibrate. The weld had all but burned through. Next, gasoline began to leak into the *cockpit*. Earhart knew she had to reach land soon.

Finally, she sighted a fishing vessel. She knew she was at the Irish coast. She followed a railroad track and landed in a meadow near Londonderry. She had crossed the Atlantic in 15

Earhart received a hero's welcome in Londonderry, Ireland, after completing her record-breaking flight.

hours and 18 minutes—faster than anyone on record—and she had done it alone.

The story of Earhart's flight quickly made the news. Britain's King George V sent the royal family's congratulations. Once Earhart arrived in England, she was given many awards and honors. Then, back in the United States, she was presented with a National Geographic gold medal by President Herbert Hoover. Earhart's acceptance speech was modest. "I hope the flight has meant something to women in aviation," she said. "If it has I shall feel justified. I can't claim anything else."

Earhart's accomplishment meant a great deal to the whole world, but especially to women. Although she was already well known, this flight demonstrated that women could set their own course in *aviation,* as well as in other careers. The Atlantic flight was certainly not Earhart's first accomplishment, and it was far from her last.

Six-year-old Amelia Earhart holds hands with her younger sister, Muriel, on the porch of their grandparents' house in Atchison, Kansas.

2

The Girl Who
Walks Alone

Born in a small town on the Mississippi River, Amelia Earhart was no stranger to the pioneer tradition. Her hometown of Atchison, Kansas, was once on the wild frontier. In fact, the town had grown out of one man's ferryboat business, which helped settlers get their wagons across the river on their way west. By 1858, a steamboat served the town, and the railroad was making its way there.

In the 1860s, Indians still made up a large part of the population in Kansas. However, the buffalo were quickly disappearing, shot for sport by people coming into the territory. Buffalo bones littered the ground along the railroad tracks.

Both of Amelia's grandfathers were in Atchison by 1861, when the Civil War broke out. Her mother's father, Alfred Otis, and her father's father, David Earhart, witnessed many scuffles and gunfights over the slavery issue. Alfred Otis was an abolitionist (a person opposed to slavery). He smuggled many runaway slaves to safety in his wagon by covering them with grain. He also brought children to freedom by hiding them in trunks as part of his luggage.

Despite the conflicts over slavery, the Otises led a good life. When Amelia's mother, Amy, was born in 1869, the Otises were quite wealthy. Alfred had a law practice, and the family enjoyed a very comfortable home on the bluffs known as Quality Hill. From their front door, they could see the bustling town of Atchison and the fast-moving Mississippi River.

The Earharts were less fortunate. In fact, they were rather poor. David Earhart and his wife, Mary, both farmers, worked long hours, but drought, dust storms, and locusts seemed to get the better of their crops. David also taught school and preached on Sundays. He was not discouraged by his poverty. In fact, he hoped that his son Edwin would become a *clergyman*. Instead, Edwin chose law.

Coming from a poor family, Edwin had to work his way through school. He did odd jobs and tutored his fellow students. He was a charming young man—funny, bright, and good-looking.

In 1890, Edwin met the woman he wanted to marry. His college roommate, Mark Otis, invited Edwin to his sister Amy's "coming out" ball. Edwin and Amy danced the night away and were soon engaged. However, Amy's father, now a judge, did not approve of Edwin Earhart. Judge Otis wanted a wealthy and ambitious husband for his daughter. He told young Edwin that he had to find a job that would earn him at least $50 a month before he could marry Amy.

Edwin Earhart found that job with the railroad, settling insurance claims. He and Amy married in 1894. They then moved into a home in Kansas City that was bought and furnished by Judge Otis.

Amy loved her husband very much, but she missed him when he went on trips for the railroad. She moved back to her parents' home in Atchison, so she would not be lonely. There, Amy gave birth to a daughter on July 24, 1897. The baby was named Amelia Mary, after her two grandmothers. Soon after, another daughter followed, named Muriel.

Amy began traveling with Edwin, and the two young girls stayed at the Otis house. Amelia and Muriel found fun and adventure on the grounds overlooking the Mississippi. They raced down to the river, searched for arrowheads, and pretended to be pioneers and Indians.

The two sisters were very close. Amelia was known as Millie, and Muriel was called Pidge. They were also close to their parents, who encouraged their daughters' curiosity and love of adventure. Amy read to them and took them on nature outings. She let them collect worms, moths, and toads. She even allowed them to wear bloomers—some of the first pants that girls were permitted to wear. Neighbors were shocked.

Edwin encouraged his daughters to take part in activities usually left to boys. He played ball with them and took them fishing. He also

Amy and Edwin Earhart allowed their tomboy daughters, Amelia and Muriel, to wear trousers and play such "unfeminine" games as baseball.

sang and played the piano with his two little tomboys. One year Amelia wrote to him requesting footballs for Christmas. "We have plenty of baseballs and bats," she explained. The girls got their wish.

In 1904, Edwin took his family to the World's Fair in St. Louis. There, Amelia got a taste of roller coasters. When she got home, she designed and built her own with the help of an uncle. Soon she was racing down its tracks. "It's just like flying!" the young daredevil yelled—right before she crashed. Amelia extended her track and enjoyed a few more runs before the frightened grown-ups made her take it down.

In 1908, Edwin took a new job with the railroad, and the family moved to Des Moines, Iowa. Here the girls had no barn to play in and no cousins to keep them company. But they still had fun. That year they went to the Iowa State Fair, where Amelia saw her first airplane.

It had been only five years since the Wright brothers had made their pioneering flight at Kitty Hawk, North Carolina. Airplanes were still crude machines. Amelia was certainly not impressed with the plane she saw. "It was a thing of rusty wire and wood and not at all interesting," she later said.

The Earhart family was very happy during the children's early years. But Edwin began to struggle, trying to live up to Judge Otis's expectations. In trying to make his fortune, Edwin began making bad business decisions. Then, he started to drink. His drinking problem became so bad that he lost his job and had a hard time finding another. He lost one job after another, and whenever he did find work, he had to move his family. Each move forced the girls to change schools. Eventually, Amy took her daughters to Chicago, where the three of them lived with some friends. Edwin stayed with his sister in Kansas City.

By this time, Amelia was 17 and in high school. Her father's alcoholism and her parents' separation were very hard on her. Moving so often made it difficult to have close friends, but she learned to get along on her own and grew into a confident young woman.

Amelia was both independent and outspoken. She complained to her mother about how boys were favored over girls. She thought girls should try to do everything boys did. Amelia would later write, "Women must try to do things as men have tried. When they fail, their failure must be but a challenge to others."

In Chicago, Amelia proved to be a good student, but she cared little about grades. She studied hard because she wanted to, not to impress her teachers. She continued her athletic habits and played on her school's basketball team. But she also had a reputation for being a loner—not because she was shy but because she was extremely serious and self-reliant. For example, when she decided her English teacher was not doing a very good job, Amelia took to studying on her own in the library.

People thought Amelia's behavior was odd. Her picture in the Hyde Park High School yearbook was captioned, "The girl in brown who walks alone." When it came time to graduate, in 1915, Amelia missed the ceremony: she simply did not show up.

Meanwhile, Amelia's father was still in Kansas City. By 1915, he had started a law prac-

Amelia, shown here at age 17, was independent and self-motivated. The caption under her high school yearbook picture read, "The girl in brown who walks alone."

tice and stopped drinking, so Amy brought their two daughters from Chicago and joined him.

Amelia lived with her parents for a year. During this time, Amy Earhart was trying to win a court battle. Her mother had died in 1911, leaving an estate worth more than $1 million. But because Mrs. Otis knew of Edwin's alcoholism, she had made arrangements for Amy's share to be placed in a bank account, where it would stay for 20 years—or until Edwin was dead.

Edwin convinced Amy to take the matter to court, as Amy's inheritance was much needed. The girls wanted to go to college, but Edwin was not making enough money to send them. Because Amy's brother Mark, who was in charge of her inheritance, was handling the account so badly, the court awarded Amy the money.

Mark had surely made some bad investment decisions: what should have been $250,000 was now only $60,000. Luckily for Amelia and Muriel, there was still plenty of money for college. Muriel chose to attend St. Margaret's in Toronto, Canada. Amelia entered the Ogontz School, a two-year college for women, near Philadelphia. This school emphasized art and literature.

As always, Amelia was very studious and adventurous. Her headmistress at Ogontz later wrote, "Amelia was always pushing into unknown seas in her reading." She retained her independent spirit, quitting her sorority after deciding that such groups were snobbish and elitist. She also kept a scrapbook of women who had become lawyers, fire lookouts, and bank presidents, or who had challenged female stereotypes in other ways.

Amelia filled her days with lectures, visits to the opera, art classes, tennis, horseback riding, and volunteer work for the Red Cross. Her attitude toward education was different from that of most young women. Instead of viewing college as a stepping-stone to marriage, Amelia thought of it as preparation for a career.

A beaming Earhart poses in her flying gear, which included a leather jacket, flying helmet, and goggles.

3

Her First
Devil Machine

During Christmas of 1917, world events made Amelia's outlook even more serious. She went to Toronto to spend time with her sister, and there she saw many Canadian soldiers who had been wounded in the war. The United States had entered World War I the previous spring, but Canada had been in the war since 1914. Seeing the suffering of the wounded soldiers was a shock.

"There for the first time I realized what

world war meant," she wrote later. "Instead of new uniforms and brass bands I saw only the results of four years' desperate struggle; men without arms and legs, men who were paralyzed and men who were blind. One day I saw four one-legged men at once, walking as best they could down the street together."

Instead of finishing her last year at college, Amelia returned to Canada to nurse the wounded soldiers. After completing a first-aid course with the Red Cross, Amelia was assigned to Toronto's Spadina Military Hospital as a nurse's aid. Amelia worked exhausting 10-hour shifts. She scrubbed floors, washed trays, worked in the kitchen, and spent time with the soldiers. She entertained them by playing the piano.

Some of the patients who became her friends were British and French pilots. One day, one of these pilots decided to play a trick on Amelia and one of her friends. The two young women were visiting an airfield. When the pilot saw them from his plane, he put the plane into a dive and aimed straight at them. Amelia's friend ran for her life, but Amelia stood still and watched the plane get closer and closer. She felt both fear and pleasure. It was then, Amelia wrote in her book *Last Flight*, that she decided to ride "one of these devil machines."

But Amelia did not think of becoming a pilot. Because of her experiences in Toronto, she decided to study medicine. She continued to work at the hospital even after the war ended in November of 1918. An influenza epidemic broke out, and her help was needed.

Unfortunately, the long hours took a toll, and Amelia became ill. She had to spend the

Earhart worked in a Toronto hospital during a flu epidemic, which killed 15 million people around the world.

spring of 1919 recovering from sinusitis—an inflammation of the nasal passages. This illness would affect her all her life. Today, sinusitis is treated with antibiotics, but at that time there was no medicine for it. The treatment involved flushing out the sinuses, which was very uncomfortable.

In the fall, Amelia signed up for a heavy load of classes at Columbia University and Barnard College in New York City. According to a friend, this difficult course schedule was "a three-man job." When she was not studying or attending classes, she went to concerts and poetry readings. She also enjoyed hiking with her friends.

In the summer of 1920, Amelia received a letter from her parents. They were living in Los Angeles and wanted her to join them. They suggested she finish her studies on the West Coast. Amelia left New York, thinking she would return in the fall. She told Muriel, "I'm going to come back here and live my own life." But out in California, at an airfield near Los Angeles,

Amelia's life took a new direction.

Ever since the war, airfields had been springing up around Los Angeles. Aviation was still new at the time, and air shows were very popular. At these shows, people crowded the fields to watch army pilots do stunts in old warplanes.

Amelia went to her first show with her father. She was so intrigued by flying that she asked him to find out about lessons. He did, but the price was too high for the Earharts. Local pilots charged $1,000 to teach a student to fly.

Just a few days later, Amelia paid a pilot one dollar for a 10-minute ride over Los Angeles. "By the time I had gotten two or three hundred feet off the ground," she wrote later, "I knew I had to fly."

From that moment on, Amelia was committed to flying, regardless of the price. She signed up for lessons, and to pay for them she got a job sorting mail at the telephone company. After working all week, she headed out to the airfield on the weekend.

Most *aviators* were men, and Amelia did not want to seem too out of place. She cut her hair and wore *breeches*, boots, and a man's leather jacket. But Amelia's instructor was a woman named Anita "Neta" Snook—the first woman to graduate from the Curtiss School of Aviation.

Amelia had to learn all about the plane, a Curtiss Canuck biplane, before she could take to the air. The plane was a trainer. Her instructor sat in the rear cockpit and from there could correct anything Amelia did.

With Neta behind her, Amelia practiced her takeoffs and landings. Then she learned some stunt-flying techniques. Knowing how to "stunt" is important to pilots because it prepares them for emergencies. According to Amelia, in her book *Last Flight,* "Unless a pilot has actually recovered from a stall, has actually put his plane into a spin and brought it out, he cannot know accurately what these acts entail."

When she was not flying, she spent time

Earhart and her flying instructor, Neta Snook (left), prepare to board a Kinner Airster biplane at a Los Angeles airport in 1920.

with all the pilots and asked questions. A class on automobile-engine repair that she had taken years before now came in handy. But there was still much to learn.

When it came time for her solo, Amelia went up 5,000 feet. She "played around a little and came back." She was thrilled. "It's so breath-takingly beautiful up there, I want to fly whenever I can," she wrote. She celebrated her flight by purchasing a leather flying coat. It was so shiny and new that Amelia received a lot of teasing. To "age" it, she stained it and slept in it.

Amelia signed up for advanced lessons, and she started saving money for her own plane.

She wanted to do nothing but fly. Her father thought flying was dangerous and foolish, but her mother was enthusiastic, even after Amelia had made two crash landings. She said that when Amelia did things, "she always did them very carefully."

In 1922, Amelia took her savings, as well as her mother's and sister's savings, and bought her first devil machine—a bright yellow Kinner Canary. But fuel was so expensive that she could not fly whenever she wanted. Amelia had to work and save. She worked part-time for her father and had several other jobs as well.

In October 1922, Edwin Earhart accompanied his two daughters to Rogers Field. That day, Amelia handed two tickets to her father and sister and ran off. She said she could not sit with them but did not explain why. They soon learned the reason after seeing Amelia disappear into the clouds in her yellow Canary. An hour later, when the plane reappeared and landed, the field's loudspeakers announced that Amelia

Earhart had broken the women's altitude record. She had climbed 14,000 feet.

The record was soon overtaken by another woman, and Amelia tried to break the new record, too. However, this time she met a dense bank of clouds and snow. Then the snow turned to sleet. She had to descend before the plane froze up. She sent the plane into a downward spin, right through a deep fog. Luckily, the fog had not descended to the ground, so Amelia was able to see clearly enough to pull her plane out of its dive. It was a frightening experience, but she did not let the men on the field know how scared she had been.

Around this time, Earhart received a pilot's license from the Fédération Aéronautique Internationale. She was one of the few women in the world licensed to fly.

For a while, Amelia was feeling wonderful, accomplishing all the things she had set out to do. But things soon changed. The Earhart family lost a lot of money in a bad investment, and Edwin and Amy decided to divorce.

Amelia sold her plane and bought a car. She and her mother would join Muriel, who was studying at Harvard. Instead of taking the train, they drove across the continent. At the time, it was quite an adventure because there were no interstate highways and few places to have a car repaired.

As soon as Amelia had settled into a house in Boston with her sister and mother, she entered the hospital. Her sinusitis had once again flared up, and she needed surgery. Doctors removed a piece of bone from her nose to allow better drainage. Finally, Amelia was free of pain.

For the next year, in trying to decide on a career, Amelia changed her mind many times. She desperately needed a job but could not find anything that suited her. Finally, in the fall of 1926, she answered an advertisement for the position of "*novice*" social worker at Denison House, a community center. She got the job and tackled it with her usual enthusiasm.

In this new job, Earhart worked with poor immigrant families. She taught English and conducted other classes, took people to the hospital when they were sick, and organized events, such as games and plays.

Soon, however, Amelia was looking toward the sky. She joined the Boston chapter of the National Aeronautic Association and was able to fly now and then. She also invested in a new airport being built in Boston. Called the Denison Airport (but not related to Denison House), it had a flying school and very good runways. Her involvement with Denison Airport got her name in the paper. Soon she was being described as "one of the best women pilots in the United States."

In April 1928, Earhart received a phone call that would change her life. It was from Captain Hilton Railey, who wanted to know if Amelia would like to be the first woman to fly across the Atlantic.

Earhart (left) meets explorer Richard Byrd and Amy Guest, the sponsor of the 1928 transatlantic flight. Guest wanted to make the trip herself but was persuaded to select an "American girl of the right image" instead.

4

"An American Girl"

When Captain Railey asked her if she wanted to fly over the Atlantic, Earhart could not believe what she had heard. Was it a joke? She demanded to know who this man was. Railey told her he ran a public relations firm. Some of his clients were aviators, such as Ruth Nichols and polar explorer Richard E. Byrd.

Later that day, Amelia Earhart took a friend along and met with Railey at a Boston hotel. There, she was told that a woman named

Amy Guest had bought Richard Byrd's plane, a *trimotor* Fokker. Guest was American born and had married an Englishman. She wanted the plane flown across the Atlantic as a show of goodwill between the United States and Great Britain. She insisted that "an American girl of the right image" be included in the flight.

Captain Railey asked Earhart if she would like to be that "American girl." Doing her best to remain calm, Amelia barely showed any excitement and said yes.

Next, Earhart had to interview with Railey's associates in New York. There, she met with publisher George Palmer Putnam, attorney David T. Layman, and another man, John Phipps. They asked her question after question about her education, work, and hobbies.

Two days later, Earhart got a letter from Layman. She had been selected for the flight. Earhart would be the commander of the flight, but she would not be the pilot of the plane. She had no experience handling multiengined planes or flying with instruments. However, if the weather was fair, Earhart would be given a turn at the controls.

The adventure was to be kept secret until the plane's takeoff. Everyone agreed that if word got out, competition might follow. Someone might beat Earhart to the distinction of being the first woman to cross the Atlantic by plane.

The plane, named the *Friendship* by Amy Guest, was in a hangar at East Boston airport. There, it awaited the fitting of pontoons (flotation devices that were used instead of wheels). The plane was painted orange and was larger than any in which Earhart had yet flown. Its golden wings, which spanned 72 feet, impressed Earhart as "strong and exquisitely fashioned." The cabin was crowded with two large gas tanks and a *navigation* table. There were no passenger seats.

While work on the *Friendship* continued, Earhart met with the pilots, Wilmer Stultz and Louis "Slim" Gordon, to plan their departure.

The *Friendship* would leave Boston for Trepassey Bay, Newfoundland, during mid-May 1928, one year after Charles Lindbergh's flight (Lindbergh was the first pilot to complete a solo flight across the Atlantic).

Unfortunately, on the scheduled departure day, fog covered all of Boston like a blanket. The weather did not clear until June 3. At dawn that day, the *Friendship* soared into the sky. It headed for Trepassey, where it would be refueled for the flight across the Atlantic.

Stultz was at the controls, and Gordon sat next to him. Earhart had to crouch down in a space behind the fuel tanks. She wore a helmet and goggles, a brown leather jacket, breeches, and boots.

After the plane got into the air, George Putnam called a news conference. Suddenly, the word was out: an American woman had just left the United States and was headed for England— by air! Reporters went to the Earhart house in Medford, demanding information about Amelia.

Amy Earhart did not know anything about the trip.

Meanwhile, Amelia Earhart was taking notes in the *Friendship*'s logbook:

> *7 o'clock. Slim has the controls and Bill is turning in. I squat on the floor.*
>
> *The sea looks like the back of an elephant, the same kind of wrinkles. . . .*

Bad weather forced the plane to land at Halifax, Nova Scotia. It arrived in Trepassey on June 4. It was met by a number of boats, crowded with cheering fishermen. Once on land, Earhart wired her mother, asking her not to worry. Amy Earhart wired back: "We are not worrying. Wish I were with you. Good Luck and cheerio. Love, Mother."

Amy Earhart waits by her radio for news of her daughter's historic flight across the ocean.

At Trepassey, the *Friendship* was again grounded by bad weather. Finally, after two weeks of waiting, the crew took off on June 17. For the next 20 hours and 40 minutes, Earhart knelt at the chart table. She filled the log with notes on the weather, airspeeds, altitudes, and compass markings. Between these entries and time spent gazing out the window, she wrote more personal notes.

"I think I am happy," she wrote. "I am getting housemaid's knee kneeling here at the table gulping beauty."

At one point, flying at 11,000 feet, the plane ran into a bank of clouds "piled like fantastic gobs of mashed potatoes." Stultz nosed the plane down. He did not want to spend precious fuel climbing above the clouds.

Near the end of the flight, storms and heavy fog closed in on the plane. By the time the sun came up, the radio was dead. The *Friendship* had only one hour's supply of fuel, and the pilot was unsure of the plane's position.

Stultz sighted an ocean liner below. Quickly, Earhart scribbled a note, asking the ship's crew to paint its position in big letters on its deck. She put the message in a bag, weighted it with an orange, and dropped it through the hatch. But the sack fell unnoticed into the sea.

Finally, they spotted fishing boats below, and beyond them a solid blue shadow. It was land! Stultz brought the plane down in a small harbor. They had landed in Burry Port, Wales.

When the crew was finally brought to shore, Hilton Railey, who had flown from London, was there to meet them.

"Congratulations!" he shouted to Ear-

A crowd gathers in Burry Port, Wales, to view the Friendship *after its arrival from America.*

hart. "How does it feel to be the first woman to have flown the Atlantic?"

"Like a sack of potatoes," she said, smiling. "Bill did all the flying. I was just baggage."

Amelia Earhart became an instant celebrity. In London, she received a note of congratulations from U.S. president Calvin Coolidge. Leading Britons such as future prime minister Winston Churchill requested her company. Earhart was swamped with requests for interviews.

After getting much attention from crowds of well-wishers in London, the three crew members of the *Friendship* set off for the United States—this time aboard an ocean liner called the *President Roosevelt*. Before Earheart left, however, she bought a small plane, an Avro Avian Moth, from Lady Mary Heath and

Earhart was often compared to aviator Charles Lindbergh (shown here), the first person to fly solo across the Atlantic. Some people referred to her as the Lady Lindy.

arranged for it to be shipped home. Heath was one of England's outstanding women pilots. In this particular plane, she had made the first solo flight from South Africa to Egypt.

As soon as the ship docked in New York, Earhart and her crew were whisked away. They received medals and keys to the city. Then they were paraded down Broadway in an open car, where they were met by cheering crowds throwing confetti. Amelia had become America's flying sweetheart.

People began calling Amelia Earhart the Lady Lindy (the female version of Charles Lindbergh). Earhart was embarrassed by the comparison. Lindbergh had made the first solo flight across the Atlantic in 1927. He had been courageous, and people loved him for it. But Amelia felt that on her great adventure she had just been a passenger. Earhart was not satisfied with riding in the backseat. She had goals of her own—such as flying the Atlantic in her own plane, alone.

Wilmer Stultz, Amelia Earhart, and "Slim" Gordon wave to New Yorkers during a parade welcoming them home after their 1928 flight to Wales.

5

Fame and
Fortune

During the crush of attention that came with Earhart's newfound fame, publisher George Putnam was always nearby. He had a gift for making celebrities, and Amelia Earhart was one of them. He became very involved in her life, advising her on what interviews to do. Because Amelia was so overwhelmed by all the attention from the public, his advice and guidance were much appreciated.

Putnam offered Earhart a contract to write a book about her part in the flight. He even offered a place to work—his own home, shared with his wife and two young sons. Soon Amelia was hard at work on the book, which would be called *20 Hrs. 40 Min.*

There were other opportunities as well. *Cosmopolitan* magazine offered Earhart a regular column on aviation. It was her chance to speak to young women about their careers. She happily accepted the job.

When her book was finished, Amelia set off in her Avian Moth for California. She visited her father and attended the National Air Races. Then she flew back to New York. With this trip, Earhart set a new aviation record: she was the first woman to make a round-trip solo flight between the nation's East and West coasts.

According to Earhart, all she "wished to do in the world was to be a vagabond—in the air." She was dreaming of new records. But she needed money to make such flights. To earn the money, she had to go on a lecture tour, which Putnam arranged. For the next year, she toured the country, speaking in as many as 27 cities in one month.

During this time, she was also writing for *Cosmopolitan*. Her articles included "Try Flying Yourself!", "Is It Safe To Fly?", and "Why Are Women Afraid To Fly?" Fan letters poured in for Amelia, asking questions about careers and marriage. Women wanted advice from this brave and thoughtful female pioneer. To them, Earhart represented the independent spirit of modern womanhood.

In the summer of 1929, Earhart sold her Avian Moth and bought a more powerful plane, a Lockheed Vega. She flew it to Santa Monica, California, and entered the Women's Air Derby. The winner of this competition would receive $2,500.

Twenty aviators participated. Among them were the most well known women fliers of the time, such as Ruth Nichols and Louise

Thaden (holder of the women's speed record). They were scheduled to fly 300 miles each day for nine days, from Santa Monica to Cleveland, Ohio. Each day, they would take off in a certain order and fly guided by only compasses and road maps.

Fifteen pilots made it to Cleveland. Thaden was first, Gladys O'Donnell came in second, and Earhart finished third. Of the five that did not make it, one lost her life. Marvel Crosson, a young pilot from Alaska, experienced engine trouble over Arizona. She bailed out, but her parachute failed to open. She fell to her death. This accident was a tragic reminder of how dangerous aviation could be.

Three months after the derby, some of the participants formed an all-female aviation society. Its first members were 99 licensed women pilots, and its name was the Ninety-Nines. Earhart was the group's first president. The group wanted to expand opportunities for women in aviation. One goal was a trip that would show the world that women could be skillful pilots. This trip was a solo flight across the Atlantic.

Ruth Nichols was one of the fliers most determined to try the solo trip. But her attempts were ended by bad weather and then a plane crash, which she survived.

Amelia Earhart also wanted to try the solo trip across the Atlantic, but she still felt too inexperienced. She needed more training. She began taking navigational instruction from weather expert James "Doc" Kimball. From then on, whenever she made a long flight, Earhart never left the ground without getting a weather clearance from Kimball.

Meanwhile, much was going on in Amelia's personal life. In the fall of 1930, her father found out he had stomach cancer. There was nothing doctors could do for him. Amelia flew out to California to be with him. He died a week later.

George Putnam, who had divorced his wife in 1929, wanted Earhart to marry him. She refused him five times, thinking that marriage might feel like a cage. She was afraid it would interfere with her career plans. But when Putnam proposed a sixth time, Earhart finally accepted. Amelia was surprised by how content she was in marriage. "I am much happier," she wrote her mother, "than I expected I could ever be in that state."

When speaking to women's groups across the country, Earhart talked about marriage. She encouraged women to do more than take care of the home. She also spoke out on the husband's role. "Marriage is a mutual responsibility and I cannot see why husbands shouldn't share in the responsibility of the home." A dedicated *feminist*, Earhart spoke out for women's rights and protested laws that discriminated against women.

Edwin Earhart stayed in close touch with his famous daughter after the family was torn apart by his alcoholism. His death in 1930 was a heavy blow to Amelia.

George Putnam was now promoting Earhart's career more than ever before. He encouraged her to write a second book, *The Fun of It*. He also arranged for her sponsorship of certain products. There was Amelia Earhart luggage, women's clothing, and stationery. He never discouraged her from having a career, and he knew he could not change her mind once she had decided to do something.

One day at breakfast, she lowered her newspaper and said, "Would you mind if I flew the Atlantic?" He knew there was no need to reply: she had made up her mind. Amelia was determined to be the first woman to fly across the ocean alone. There was nothing to do but help with the preparations.

On May 21, 1932, Amelia Earhart's dream came true. She had flown the Atlantic solo and was the first woman to do so. Now when people congratulated her, she could feel that she had earned their praise. But best of all was how she felt about herself. She had set her goal and accomplished it, and she felt great.

"To want in one's own heart to do a thing for its own sake," she wrote, "to concentrate all one's energies upon it—that is not only the surest guarantee of success, it is also being true to oneself."

This flight made Earhart more famous than ever. There were banquets, parades, various awards and honors, and press interviews. When her husband arrived in England aboard an ocean liner, they traveled to France and Italy and were greeted by government leaders and the pope. They were mobbed whenever they appeared in public. On June 15, Amelia and George sailed for the United States. Their ship was escorted to sea by airplanes that dropped flowers and dipped their wings to salute the famous aviator on board.

Back home, Amelia and George attended a ceremony in Washington, D.C. Amelia entered Constitution Hall on the arm of

In 1931, Earhart married George Putnam. Amelia had turned him down five times before because she regarded marriage as at best "an attractive cage." She was pleased to discover that she enjoyed marriage to Putnam, who did not try to stop her from making her own decisions.

President Herbert Hoover. President Hoover made a speech to the distinguished audience. He said that Earhart had wanted "to help others share in the rich opportunities in life" and that she had worked to "enlarge those opportunities by expanding the powers of women." The next day, the U.S. Congress held a special session and voted to make Amelia Earhart the first woman ever to receive the Distinguished Flying Cross.

After these ceremonies, Earhart went on to break more records. She set a new women's long-distance record by flying nonstop from Los Angeles to Newark, New Jersey, in 19 hours and

5 minutes. Eleven months later, she broke this record herself. She made the trip in 17 hours and 7 1/2 minutes.

In 1932, Earhart published *The Fun of It.* This book contained information about the growing field of aviation. It also had short biographies of other women fliers. The book was a great success.

There was no doubt that America was in love with Amelia Earhart. She and George were often invited to the White House by the Roosevelts. Amelia and Eleanor Roosevelt, the first lady, became good friends. Once, at a formal dinner party, Amelia discovered that Eleanor had never been for a ride in a plane. Right away, Amelia made some calls and borrowed a plane. Soon she and the first lady were flying high over Washington, D.C., wearing their long evening gowns and white gloves.

At the age of 37, Earhart was at the height of her career. But she was restless. She wanted some new adventure. She wanted to do something no one, man or woman, had ever done before. The challenge she chose was a dangerous 2,400-mile flight between Hawaii and California. It was a complicated flight that would test Earhart's navigational skills.

Amelia and George moved to California, and Amelia bought a new plane with navigational equipment. To help her prepare for the flight, she enlisted the help of a friend, Paul Mantz, who was a highly skilled stunt pilot and expert navigator.

Amelia loved California. In between preparations for her flight, she entertained movie stars Mary Pickford and Douglas Fairbanks, comedian Will Rogers, and many other celebrities. She played golf, swam, and enjoyed the sunshine.

Earhart often visited First Lady Eleanor Roosevelt (right) at the White House and once took her flying.

In late December 1934, Earhart set sail for Hawaii with Mantz and her husband. On board the ship was her new Vega. The public was unaware of Amelia's plan, but when she arrived in Honolulu with her plane, her intentions were clear.

Not everyone was excited by this new adventure. Just one month before, American pilot Charles Ulm had been lost while attempting a flight from California to Hawaii. A search was conducted for 27 days, but he was never found. Earhart's flight was considered dangerous and pointless. There were other criticisms, too, but Amelia would not be stopped—not even by the weather.

Heavy rains came on the morning of January 11, the date of her departure. There was some doubt that Amelia would be able to take off, and more storms were on the way. In the afternoon, she boarded her plane and prepared to leave. She had three tons to lift off the ground, but she was determined to try. As the plane moved down the runway, Mantz ran alongside it shouting, "Get that tail up!" She did as he said and then lifted off. Once in the air, Earhart climbed above the clouds to a blue sky.

By midnight, Earhart was flying in rain. She flew on through the night, and then, at last, she saw light on the horizon. In the final hours of the flight, fog enveloped the plane. Then, glancing down through a hole in the fog, she saw a ship. She dove down fast, from 8,000 to 200 feet, to get a better look. The ship was bound for San Francisco, which was only 300 miles away.

After 18 hours and 15 minutes in the air, Earhart landed at the Oakland, California, airport. She was met by 10,000 people. At first, the crowd did not realize who had landed. Then, everyone ran to the plane and showered the famous pilot with roses. Amelia Earhart had set another record. "I feel swell," she said.

The following spring, Earhart was invited by the president of Mexico to visit his country in her plane. She accepted. She would go from Los Angeles to Mexico City, then fly across the Gulf of Mexico and ultimately land in New Jersey.

One friend, pilot Wiley Post, tried to convince her not to make the trip. Earhart's response revealed her pioneering spirit. In her eyes, Wiley Post had "braved every sort of hazard in his stratosphere flying." If he thought this

Ten thousand people mob Earhart's plane upon her arrival in Oakland after her solo flight from Hawaii on January 12, 1935.

trip was too hazardous, then Amelia "could scarcely wait" to be on her way. She wanted to do what the bravest of men thought dangerous.

On April 19, 1935, Earhart took off from Burbank, California. Fifty miles short of Mexico, she landed in a pasture, not knowing where she was. Some farmers pointed her in the right direction, and she took off. Her husband and the president of Mexico welcomed her when she arrived in Mexico City. After many parties celebrating her flight, she took off for Newark, New Jersey—2,185 miles away. When she landed there, she was mobbed by a crowd of admirers.

Earhart was now confident in her abilities and wanted to prove that women could be bold and courageous leaders. She began thinking of an adventure that would outdo everything any pilot had ever done. She would need a bigger plane, one with more than one motor—one that could take her around the world!

Earhart says good-bye to her husband before departing on her trip around the world.

6

The World Adventure

In 1935, Amelia Earhart accepted a part-time position at Purdue University in Lafayette, Indiana. She agreed to spend one month each year at the university as an aeronautical adviser and women's career counselor. She also continued making speeches around the country.

While Earhart was in between adventures, her friend Wiley Post was making a flight to the Arctic Circle with Will Rogers. Post had already made a couple of flights around the world, going solo the second time. But the Arctic flight ended in tragedy. On August 15, 1935, Post's plane crashed in a fog over Alaska, killing both Post and Rogers.

Amelia was shocked by the disaster, but she did not let it change her own flight plans. She spent every free minute she had with Paul Mantz, practicing flying "blind" with only navigational instruments to guide her, to prepare for situations with poor visibility.

In April 1936, Purdue University purchased a Lockheed Electra for Earhart so that

Humorist Will Rogers (left) and aviator Wiley Post relax before taking off for the Arctic Circle. On August 15, 1935, Post's plane crashed in Alaska, and both men were killed.

she could continue learning about aviation. On July 22, she flew the plane for the first time. It was a sleek, silver plane of the latest design, equipped with the most sophisticated instruments available. Its tanks held enough fuel for a 4,500-mile flight. After testing the plane, Earhart told the press that she was "nearly sold on this idea of flying around the world."

Many of Earhart's friends were not so enthusiastic about the idea. They tried to discourage her from making such a dangerous trip. Amelia responded, "If I should pop off, it will be doing the thing I've always wanted to do."

In her book *Last Flight,* Earhart tried to explain herself: "Here was my belief, that now and then women should do for themselves what men have already done—and occasionally what men have not done." By doing so, she said, women could establish themselves "as persons," and then perhaps they could also encourage "other women toward greater independence of thought and action."

Although Post had flown around the world, no woman had ever done it. Also, no one had ever flown the earth at its "waist," or near the equator. This would be Earhart's route.

In March 1937, along with Paul Mantz and two navigators, Earhart left Oakland, California, for Hawaii. The flight was the first leg of the world trip. The next leg, to Howland Island in the mid-Pacific, never happened. As the plane rolled down the runway, one wing dipped, sending the plane in a swerve. Landing gear broke free, and gas sprayed out of the plane. Earhart reacted quickly and cut the engines, preventing the plane from bursting into flame. No lives were lost, but the plane was badly damaged. It was taken back to Los Angeles for repairs.

Because of seasonal weather changes, a new route was planned. Earhart would fly from California to Florida, then to South America. She would cross the Atlantic Ocean, fly across Africa, India, and Southeast Asia, then go on to Australia, the Pacific island of New Guinea, and

Howland Island. From there, she would go on to Honolulu and finally to Oakland.

It would be an expensive adventure. The repairs to the Electra cost more than $25,000. Amelia and George spent most of their savings to pay for expenses. Others helped finance the trip, and George organized fund-raisers.

Earhart's support crew was growing larger. Fred Noonan, who was considered a superb *celestial* navigator, was hired to accompany Amelia on the world flight. Paul Mantz was still working as a consultant. Before her departure, he voiced great concern about the flight.

Mantz felt that Earhart was spending too much time fund-raising instead of preparing for the trip. Also, he was very much alarmed when he found that she had ordered the removal of the Electra's 250-foot trailing radio antenna and the plane's telegraph key. Without these devices on the plane, people at ground stations and on ships would be less able to pick up messages from the plane. It would also be difficult for her to receive messages. But Earhart felt that the antenna was an annoyance. Since neither she nor Noonan knew Morse code, she decided that the key, too, was unnecessary.

Earhart and Noonan set out on June 1, 1937. For the next 32 days, news of the flight made front-page headlines around the world. Amelia sent reports to the *New York Herald Tribune.* She wrote about the terrains, cultures, and people she encountered. After arriving in Senegal, on Africa's west coast, she commented, "What have we in the United States done to these proud people, so handsome and intelligent in the setting of their own country?"

Earhart follows navigator Fred Noonan into the Electra.

On their way to Calcutta, India, Earhart and Noonan were hit by rain and winds typical of monsoon season. When they were ready to leave Calcutta, the rain had made the airfield muddy. Forecasts predicted rain and more rain, but Amelia pressed on.

The takeoff was shaky. "The plane," Earhart wrote, "clung for what seemed like ages to the heavy, sticky soil before the wheels finally lifted, and we cleared with nothing at all to spare the fringe of trees at the airdrome's edge." The rains continued, hitting the plane so hard that patches of paint came off the wings.

After several stops, Earhart landed in Darwin, Australia, on June 27. Three days later, she was in Lae, New Guinea. Earhart wrote in her logbook, "Twenty-two thousand miles have been covered so far. There are 7,000 more to go."

The next stop was Howland Island. This leg of the trip was by far the most dangerous. It was a tiny island in the vast Pacific Ocean, so finding it would be difficult. And there was another problem: Fred Noonan was an alcoholic, and the pressure of the trip was getting to him. Amelia was now doing much of the navigating, as he was very often too drunk to help.

On Howland Island, a new runway had been built. The U.S. Coast Guard cutter *Itasca* was lying offshore. It was responsible for sending radio signals to the Electra to guide it to Howland. Another cutter, the *Ontario,* was at sea, midway between Lae and Howland Island.

Before Earhart took off from Lae, there was some confusion about radio transmissions between the Electra, the weather station at Lae, and the vessels stationed in the Pacific. The *Itasca*'s radio crew warned Amelia to transmit on a particular frequency. She wired back that she would transmit on another one. The ship's radio crew did not know that the large antenna had been removed from Earhart's plane. They were also unaware that Earhart and Noonan did not know Morse code. The confusion was not cleared up before Amelia left the ground.

When they left Lae, Earhart had to help Noonan into the plane. He had been drinking the night before and now could barely function. Also, Amelia had a hard time getting the plane in the air. It was loaded with 1,150 gallons of gasoline and was hard to maneuver. Pilots who were watching the takeoff were amazed. When the plane reached the end of the jungle runway, it lifted off the ground, but its propellers hit the waves as it headed over the ocean.

About a third of the way to Howland Island, Earhart called the Lae radio station and said she was switching to another frequency for the night. The operator told her that her signal was clear and urged her not to change frequencies. Earhart switched her frequency anyway.

At 2:45 A.M. Howland Island time, Earhart reported weather conditions as cloudy. Two more transmissions came from Earhart before 6:15 A.M., and the radio operators responded immediately. "What is your position?" they asked. "When do you expect to

Earhart and Noonan had almost completed their trip around the world when their plane was lost in the South Pacific.

arrive at Howland?" But no answer came.

The Electra was scheduled to arrive at 6:30 A.M. At 6:15 A.M., Earhart transmitted again, asking for a radio bearing. Again, the radio operators lost the transmission. Suddenly, they heard her loud and clear. "Give me the weather!" she said. "I've got to know the weather!"

A new weather report had just been issued. Heavy clouds and rain were northwest of Howland. Earhart must have already run into the storm. The information was transmitted to Earhart, but again there was only silence from the Electra.

Amelia's voice was heard several more times. Coast guardsmen scanned the sky, but they could not spot her. Finally, she sent in another message: "We are on the line of position 157-337," she said. "We are running north and south." Then there was silence. The world never heard from Amelia Earhart again.

Having failed to reach the island, Earhart's plane had almost certainly run out of fuel and fallen into the ocean. But Earhart's friends clung to the slim hope that she might still be alive. One of the largest search parties in history was formed. There were 60 planes and 10 ships dispatched. The search covered 250,000 square miles, lasted two weeks, and cost $4 million. But not a trace of the plane or its crew was ever found.

People around the world were stunned by the loss of their beloved hero. Many simply refused to believe that she was gone. Strange stories began to appear about Earhart being alive and well, living in New Jersey or on a South Pacific island. Some even suggested that Earhart was actually on a secret spying mission for the

U.S. government. Because she disappeared mysteriously and was never found, people remain curious about her fate to this day.

More important than the mystery of her final voyage, however, are her many accomplishments. At a time when women were expected to take a backseat to men, Earhart proved that women could do anything men could. Whether working as a premedical student, nurse's aide, social worker, lecturer, writer, or editor, Earhart showed that a determined woman could achieve anything she set her mind to. And when her brave exploits won the admiration of millions, Earhart used her fame to advance the cause of women everywhere.

Amelia Earhart is one of the true heroes of the 20th century. She showed courage and integrity, and her independent spirit won the respect of women and men alike. Her example has inspired thousands of women to seek new horizons and new roles for themselves.

Further Reading

Backus, Jean L. *Letters from Amelia*. Boston: Beacon Press, 1982.

Blythep, Randolph. *Amelia Earhart*. New York: Watts, 1987.

Brink, Randall. *Lost Star: The Search for Amelia Earhart*. New York: Norton, 1988.

Chadwick, Roxanne. *Anne Morrow Lindbergh: Pilot and Poet*. Minneapolis: Lerner, 1987.

Collins, David R. *Charles Lindbergh, Hero Pilot*. Champaign, IL: Garrard, 1978.

Davidson, Jesse. *Famous Firsts in Aviation*. New York: Putnam, 1974.

Mondey, David. *Women of the Air*. Morristown, NJ: Silver Burdett, 1982.

Glossary

altimeter   an instrument that measures the altitude, or the height, of a plane above the ground

altitude   the distance above the ground of an object in the air

aviation   the operation and development of airplanes

aviator   pilot

breeches   short, tight pants reaching just below the knee

celestial   relating to the sky and the sun, moon, and stars; celestial navigation involves determining one's location by observing the position of the stars

clergyman   a minister of a Christian church

cockpit   the space where the pilot of an airplane sits

feminist   a supporter of women's rights

navigation   the measurement of the course, position, and distance traveled of a plane, ship, or spacecraft

novice   beginner

solo   alone

trimotor   having three motors

Chronology

July 24, 1897	Born Amelia Mary Earhart in Atchison, Kansas
1918	Serves as a nurse's aide at Spadina Military Hospital in Toronto, Canada
1919	Enrolls as a premedical student at Columbia University in New York City
1920–22	Moves to Los Angeles and begins flying lessons
Oct. 1922	Sets women's altitude record at a Los Angeles airshow
1926–28	Works as a social worker in Boston
June 18, 1928	As a passenger, becomes the first woman to fly across the Atlantic Ocean
Sept. 1928	Publishes *20 Hrs. 40 Min.*; becomes first woman to fly round-trip across the United States solo
Feb. 7, 1931	Marries George Palmer Putnam
May 21, 1932	Becomes first woman to fly the Atlantic Ocean solo
June 1, 1937	Embarks on a round-the-world flight
July 3, 1937	Plane is lost in the South Pacific

Index

Leigh Hope Wood is an editor and writer who lives in New York City. She holds a B.S. from Emory University and an M.A. in American studies from New York University. She has also written *The Navajo Indians* and *The Crow Indians* in Chelsea House's JUNIOR LIBRARY OF AMERICAN INDIANS.

PICTURE CREDITS